INSPRENEURSHIP

30 Indian Startup Stories

A. MAHESHWARI

TABLE OF CONTENT

- Paytm — 1
- Flipkart — 2
- Games24x7 — 3
- Policybazaar — 4
- Easemytrip — 5
- Razor Pay — 6
- Nykaa — 7
- Dream 11 — 8
- Cred — 9
- Unacademy — 10
- Delhivery — 11
- Meesho — 12
- Affle — 13
- Zivame — 14
- Groww — 15
- Mamaearth — 16
- Rapido — 17
- Delta Corp — 18
- Mobikwik — 19
- MPL — 20
- Pharmeasy — 21
- Lenskart — 22
- Rivigo — 23
- Upstox — 24
- Curefit — 25
- Renew Power — 26
- Mapmyindia — 27
- Rate Gain — 28
- Upgrad — 29
- Firstcry — 30

DEDICATED TO

Every child has a dream at a young age to make lots of money and to help thousands and millions of people in their lives. However, many of these dreams never come to fruition due to a lack of starting. With this in mind, this book is dedicated to children and students who want to learn from those who have accomplished their goals and are currently living their dreams. The intention is to provide inspiration, to share the difficulties that were overcome, and to encourage them to never give up on their aspirations.

This book aims to provide a source of motivation and guidance to those who are still on their journey towards achieving their dreams. It is a testament to the fact that anything is possible with hard work and determination. The stories shared in this book will serve as a reminder that even the most successful individuals have faced challenges and obstacles along the way.

It is important to understand that success is not a straight path and that there will be setbacks and difficulties. The key is to never lose sight of the end goal and to always push forward. This book will provide examples of individuals who have faced their own struggles and have come out victorious

FORWARD

It is with great pleasure that I introduce this motivational book, a collection of inspiring and motivating stories of Indian entrepreneurs who have dared to chase their dreams and turn them into reality. This book is a testament to the fact that anything is possible with hard work and determination.

As the founder of my own startup, I understand firsthand the challenges and obstacles that come with starting a new business. The journey can be filled with uncertainty, doubt, and a seemingly endless list of setbacks. However, it is important to remember that these challenges are only temporary and that success is possible.

This book is a valuable resource for anyone who is considering starting their own business or for those who are already on the journey and need a little motivation. It is a compilation of real-life stories from individuals who have faced similar challenges and have come out victorious. Through their experiences, readers will learn about the importance of perseverance, the power of a strong vision, and the role of a supportive team.

I am confident that this book will serve as a source of inspiration and guidance for anyone who is looking to turn their dream into a reality. I hope that this book with 30 short powerful startup stories will empower and inspire future entrepreneurs to chase their dreams and make a positive impact on the world.

ABOUT PAYTM

Paytm is an Indian mobile payment and financial services company that operates through a multi-sided platform business model. It provides a range of services to both consumers and merchants. The main source of revenue for Paytm comes from its mobile wallet service, where users can add money and use it to make payments for various services like mobile recharge, bill payments, online shopping and other services like movie tickets, flight tickets and bus tickets booking. Paytm also operates a payment gateway service for merchants to accept payments from customers through various channels, including credit/debit cards, net banking, and Paytm wallet.

FINTECH

Founder : Vijay Shekhar Sharma

Vijay Shekhar Sharma, the founder of Paytm, is one of the most inspiring entrepreneurs in India. He started his journey as a young boy from a small town in Uttar Pradesh, India. He grew up in a lower-middle-class family and had to struggle to make ends meet. However, despite the tough circumstances, he was determined to make something of himself.

Vijay was always fascinated by technology and had a natural inclination towards it. He completed his engineering degree from Delhi College of Engineering and started working as a software engineer. However, he soon realized that his true passion lay in entrepreneurship. He quit his job and started working on his own ventures.

In 2000, Vijay started a company called One97 Communications, which was focused on mobile content and commerce. The company struggled in its early days, and Vijay had to face many challenges. He was often short on funds and had to borrow money from friends and family to keep the company running. But, he never gave up.

In 2010, Vijay launched Paytm, a mobile wallet and e-commerce platform, which quickly gained popularity among the Indian consumers. Paytm was one of the first companies in India to introduce the concept of mobile wallets and cashless transactions. Vijay's vision was to make digital payments accessible to every Indian, especially those in rural and remote areas who had limited access to banking services.

Paytm's success was not an overnight phenomenon. Vijay and his team had to work hard to establish the company's presence in the market. They faced stiff competition from established players and had to overcome various regulatory and technical challenges. But, Vijay's determination and passion for the business kept him going.

Today, Paytm is one of the most valuable startups in India and has a user base of over 350 million. Vijay's story is a testament to the power of hard work, perseverance, and determination. He has shown that with the right attitude and a strong will, anyone can achieve their dreams, no matter where they come from or what their background is.

ABOUT FLIPKART

Flipkart is an Indian e-commerce company that operates through an online marketplace business model. The company allows vendors and sellers to list and sell their products on the platform, while it acts as an intermediary between the buyers and sellers. Flipkart generates revenue primarily through commissions and fees charged to vendors and sellers for listing and selling their products on the platform. Additionally, it also earns revenue through advertising, promoted listings and subscription services like Flipkart Plus. Flipkart also has its own private labels which it sells on the platform, that also generates revenue for the company. Flipkart also provides various services like easy return, exchange, and EMI options for the customers.

E COMMERCE

Founder : Sachin Bansal & Binny Bansal

Flipkart, founded by Sachin Bansal and Binny Bansal in 2007 while they were both working at Amazon, faced numerous challenges on its journey to becoming one of India's leading e-commerce companies. Initially, the company faced difficulty in convincing consumers to trust online shopping and make purchases through their website. Additionally, they faced stiff competition from established players in the market, such as Amazon and Snapdeal.

Despite these challenges, the founders were determined to make Flipkart a success. They focused on building a strong logistics and delivery network, as well as providing excellent customer service. They also introduced innovative features such as cash on delivery and easy returns, which helped to build trust with consumers.

One of the major challenges faced by Flipkart was the entry of Amazon in the Indian market. Amazon had much deeper pockets and a more established brand, which made it difficult for Flipkart to compete. However, the founders of Flipkart were motivated to prove that their company could stand on its own, and they redoubled their efforts to improve their offerings and customer service.

In addition to these external challenges, Flipkart also faced internal struggles, such as leadership changes and a revolving door of top executives. However, the company's founders were able to steer the company through these challenges, and Flipkart continued to grow and evolve.

Despite the difficulties, Flipkart's founders remained determined and motivated to build a successful company. Their perseverance and belief in their vision helped them overcome the challenges and turn Flipkart into one of the most valuable and successful startups in India. Today, Flipkart is a household name and a major player in the Indian e-commerce industry, known for its innovative approach and customer-centric philosophy.

ABOUT GAMES24X7

Games24x7 is an Indian online gaming company that operates through a freemium business model. It offers a wide range of games such as rummy, fantasy cricket, and fantasy football, which can be played for free or for cash. The company generates revenue primarily through in-app purchases and advertising. Players can purchase virtual currencies or other in-game items to enhance their gaming experience, and the company also earns revenue from advertising on its platform. Additionally, Games24x7 also offers subscription services for premium features and special promotions for its users. The company also operates a tournament-based model where users pay an entry fee to participate in tournaments, and the prize money is distributed among the winners.

GAMING

Founder : Bhavin Tuakhia

Games24x7, founded by Bhavin Turakhia, has raised over $15 million in funding from investors such as Matrix Partners, Lightspeed Venture Partners, and Sequoia Capital.

Bhavin Turakhia, the founder and CEO of Games24x7, is a serial entrepreneur and has a history of building successful companies. He started his first company, Directi, at the age of 18 with his brother Divyank. Directi was a successful web services company that was eventually sold for over a billion dollars. After the sale of Directi, Bhavin Turakhia decided to focus on the online gaming industry in India and founded Games24x7.

The company initially faced challenges in convincing traditional Indian investors of the potential of the online gaming industry, and had to bootstrap its way to success. Another challenge faced by Games24x7 was the legal and regulatory environment in India. At the time, the legal status of online gaming in India was uncertain and there were concerns about the potential for fraud and cheating. The company had to navigate these challenges and work to establish a reputation for fair play and transparency. Despite these difficulties, Games24x7 has grown to become one of the largest online gaming companies in India, with a particular focus on skill-based games like rummy and fantasy cricket. In 2019, the company was acquired by the Indian e-commerce giant Flipkart for an undisclosed amount.

Bhavin Turakhia's entrepreneurial journey has been remarkable, he was able to build a successful business from scratch. He is also known for his philanthropic activities, he has donated a significant amount of money to various charities and has also started his own charitable foundation.

In conclusion, the story of Games24x7 and its founder, Bhavin Turakhia, serves as an inspiration for entrepreneurs and startups. It shows that with hard work, determination, and a great idea, it is possible to build a successful business from scratch, and also how one can give back to the society.

ABOUT POLICY BAZAAR

PolicyBazaar is an Indian online insurance comparison and purchasing platform that operates through a lead generation business model. The company allows customers to compare and purchase insurance policies from a variety of providers such as health, car, life, and travel insurance. PolicyBazaar generates revenue primarily through commissions and fees charged by insurance providers for each policy purchased through the platform. Customers can compare different policies, and when they are ready to purchase, they are directed to the insurance providers' website or to the insurance provider's agent. PolicyBazaar also earns revenue through advertising, as it offers space for insurance providers and other companies to advertise their products and services on its platform. The company also provides services like EMI options and claim assistance to customers which also contributes to its revenue.

INSURANCE

Founder : Yashish Dahiya, Alok Bansal, and Avaneesh Nirjar

The story of PolicyBazaar and its founders is an interesting one. The company was founded in 2008 by Yashish Dahiya, Alok Bansal, and Avaneesh Nirjar. They had the vision to make insurance more accessible and understandable for the average consumer in India by providing them with an easy-to-use platform that compares different insurance policies and allows them to purchase the policy that best suits their needs.

Yashish Dahiya, the CEO of PolicyBazaar, is a serial entrepreneur and had previously co-founded a company called Baazee.com, which was later acquired by eBay. He has been in the e-commerce space for over a decade and has a wealth of experience in the field.

Alok Bansal, the COO of PolicyBazaar, has over 20 years of experience in the insurance and financial services sector. He has worked with companies such as ICICI Lombard and HDFC Standard Life.

Avaneesh Nirjar, the CTO of PolicyBazaar, has over 15 years of experience in the technology industry. He has worked with companies such as Baazee.com and IBM.

The founders of PolicyBazaar have built a strong and dedicated team that is committed to making insurance more accessible and understandable for the average consumer in India. Initially many people were hesitant to purchase insurance online and were not familiar with the process. PolicyBazaar had to work to educate consumers and build trust in its platform. Another challenge was the highly regulated nature of the insurance industry in India. PolicyBazaar had to navigate a complex regulatory environment and comply with strict rules and regulations.

Through their hard work and determination, PolicyBazaar has grown to become one of the leading insurance comparison websites in India. The company has raised over $200 million in funding from investors such as SoftBank, Tiger Global Management, and Info Edge. Today, PolicyBazaar has millions of registered users, and it has also expanded its services to other countries such as UAE and Saudi Arabia.

The story of PolicyBazaar and its founders is a great example of how a team of experienced and dedicated individuals can come together to build a successful business in a highly regulated and traditional industry.

ABOUT EASE MY TRIP

EaseMyTrip is an Indian online travel agency that operates through an online marketplace business model. The company allows customers to search and book a wide range of travel products and services, such as flights, hotels, and vacation packages. EaseMyTrip generates revenue primarily through commissions and fees charged to suppliers of travel products and services, such as airlines, hotels, and car rental companies, for listing and selling their products on the platform. Additionally, EaseMyTrip also earns revenue through advertising, as it offers space for travel suppliers and other companies to advertise their products and services on its platform. The company also offers various value-added services like visa and passport assistance, travel insurance and holiday packages which also generates revenue for the company.

TOURISM

Founder : Nishant Pitti

Ease My trip, listed on Indian Stock Exchange as Easy Trip Planner was founded in 2008 by Nishant Pitti, a young entrepreneur who had a vision to make travel more accessible and affordable for Indian consumers.

Nishant Pitti faced several challenges in the early days of starting Ease My trip, such as lack of awareness about the benefits of online travel booking, a lack of trust in online transactions, and competition from established players in the market like Yatra.com, makemytrip.com, ixigo.com and many others. He also faced difficulties in building a reliable and efficient technology infrastructure to support the business.

Another major challenge was the lack of funding. Nishant Pitti had to bootstrap the company in the early days and struggled to raise funding from investors. He faced rejection after rejection, but he persisted and eventually was able to secure funding from some investors. There was a legal controversy associated with its name as it is similar to make my trip.

Despite these challenges, Nishant Pitti persevered and focused on building a user-friendly platform that was easy for Indian consumers to use. He also invested in marketing and customer acquisition efforts to raise awareness about Ease My trip among Indian consumers.

Through his hard work and determination, Ease My trip has grown to become one of the leading online travel agencies in India. The company has raised over $50 million in funding from investors such as Amadeus Capital Partners, and Norwest Venture Partners.

Today, Ease My trip has millions of registered users and is considered as one of the key players in the Indian travel market.

Nishant Pitti's story show how an entrepreneur can overcome many obstacles and achieve success through hard work, determination, and a strong vision. His story serves as an inspiration for entrepreneurs and startups looking to build a successful business from scratch.

ABOUT RAZOR PAY

Razorpay is an Indian payment gateway and financial services company that operates through a multi-sided platform business model. It provides a range of services to both consumers and merchants. The main source of revenue for Razorpay comes from its payment gateway service, where merchants can use it to accept payments from customers through various channels, including credit/debit cards, net banking, and various digital wallets. Additionally, Razorpay also operates a 'RazorpayX' which is a platform for businesses to manage their payments, subscriptions, and invoicing. It also generates revenue through its 'Razorpay Capital' which is a lending service that provides working capital loans to merchants. Additionally, it earns revenue through advertising and subscriptions services like 'Razorpay Subscriptions' which help merchants in simplifying the recurring payments.

FINTECH

Founder : Harshil Mathur and Shashank Kumar

Razorpay was founded in 2014 by Harshil Mathur and Shashank Kumar, two young entrepreneurs who saw an opportunity to create a simple and easy-to-use payment gateway for businesses in India.

Harshil Mathur and Shashank Kumar faced several challenges in the early days of starting Razorpay. One of the major challenges was the lack of awareness and understanding about the benefits of online payment gateway among Indian businesses. Additionally, building a reliable and efficient technology infrastructure to support the business was a significant challenge.

Another major challenge was competition from established players in the market. The market for payment gateway providers in India was already crowded, and it was difficult for Razorpay to stand out and attract customers.

Despite these challenges, Harshil Mathur and Shashank Kumar persevered and focused on building a user-friendly platform that was easy for businesses to use. They also invested in marketing and customer acquisition efforts to raise awareness about Razorpay among Indian businesses.

Through their hard work and determination, Razorpay has grown to become one of the leading online payment gateway providers in India. The company has raised over $100 million in funding from investors such as Ribbit Capital, Sequoia India, and Matrix Partners. Today, Razorpay has millions of registered users and is considered as one of the key players in the Indian fintech market.

The story of Razorpay and its founders Harshil Mathur and Shashank Kumar, indicates how a small startup can overcome obstacles and achieve success through hard work, determination, and a strong vision. It serves as an inspiration for entrepreneurs and startups looking to build a successful business in a highly regulated and crowded industry.

ABOUT NYKAA

Nykaa is an Indian e-commerce platform that operates through an online marketplace business model. The company allows vendors and sellers to list and sell their beauty and personal care products on the platform, while it acts as an intermediary between the buyers and sellers. Nykaa generates revenue primarily through commissions and fees charged to vendors and sellers for listing and selling their products on the platform. Additionally, it also earns revenue through advertising and subscription services like Nykaa Prime. Nykaa also has its own private labels which it sells on the platform, that also generates revenue for the company. Nykaa also provides various services like easy return, exchange, and EMI options for the customers. The company also offers a wide range of beauty and personal care products such as makeup, skincare, hair care, and fragrances, as well as provides beauty advice and expert tips on its platform.

E COMMERCE

Founder : Falguni Nayar

Falguni Nayar is the founder and CEO of Nykaa, an Indian online beauty and wellness retailer. Before starting Nykaa, she had a successful career as an investment banker. She worked in a number of senior roles at companies such as Kotak Mahindra Capital, UBS and Kotak Investment Bank.

In 2012, Falguni Nayar decided to leave her successful career in investment banking and start her own business. She saw an opportunity to create an online platform that would make it easier for Indian consumers to access a wide range of beauty and wellness products. Despite having no prior experience in the e-commerce or beauty industry, she decided to take the leap and start Nykaa.

Falguni Nayar faced several challenges in the early days of starting Nykaa. She had to bootstrap the company in the early days and struggled to raise funding from investors. Additionally, building a reliable and efficient technology infrastructure to support the business was a significant challenge.

She also faced difficulty in raising funding for the business, as many investors were skeptical about the potential for an online beauty retail business in India. Despite these challenges, Falguni Nayar persevered and focused on building a user-friendly platform that was easy for Indian consumers to use. She also invested in marketing and customer acquisition efforts to raise awareness about Nykaa among Indian consumers.

Through her hard work and determination, Nykaa has grown to become one of the leading online beauty and wellness retailers in India. The company has raised over $80 million in funding from investors such as TVS Capital and TPG Growth. Today, Nykaa has millions of registered users and is considered as one of the key players in the Indian e-commerce market.

Falguni Nayar's story is a great example of how an entrepreneur can overcome many obstacles and achieve success through hard work, determination, and a strong vision. Her story serves as an inspiration for entrepreneurs and startups looking to build a successful business from scratch. It also showcases how one can change career paths and excel in a new field.

ABOUT DREAM11

Dream11 is an Indian online gaming platform that operates through a freemium business model. The company allows users to play fantasy sports games such as cricket, football, kabaddi, and basketball, which can be played for free or for cash. Dream11 generates revenue primarily through in-app purchases and advertising. Users can purchase virtual currencies or other in-game items to enhance their gaming experience, and the company also earns revenue from advertising on its platform. Additionally, Dream11 also offers subscription services for premium features and special promotions for its users. The company operates a tournament-based model where users pay an entry fee to participate in tournaments, and the prize money is distributed among the winners. The company has a strong user base and is one of the most popular online gaming platforms in India, which helps to attract more players and advertisers.

GAMING

Founder : Harsh Jain and Bhavit Sheth

Dream11, an Indian fantasy sports platform, was founded in 2008 by Harsh Jain and Bhavit Sheth.

Harsh Jain, the CEO of Dream11, is a graduate of Indian Institute of Technology (IIT) Bombay, and has a background in technology. Prior to starting Dream11, Harsh has worked with companies such as Ericsson and Reliance Entertainment.

Bhavit Sheth, the COO of Dream11, is also a graduate of IIT Bombay, and has a background in finance. Prior to starting Dream11, he has worked with companies such as ICICI Bank and Deloitte.

The founders of Dream11 faced several challenges in the early days of starting the company, such as lack of awareness about the concept of fantasy sports in India, difficulties in building a reliable and efficient technology infrastructure to support the business and struggle to raise funding from investors. Additionally, fantasy sports were not yet legalised in India and the founders had to navigate the legal complexities of operating in an unregulated market.

Through their hard work, determination, and a strong vision, Dream11 has grown to become one of the leading fantasy sports platforms in India. The company has raised over $100 million in funding from investors such as Kalaari Capital, Multiples Alternate Asset Management, and Think Investments. Today, Dream11 has millions of registered users and is considered as one of the key players in the Indian gaming market.

In 2018, Dream11 became the first Indian gaming company to enter the Unicorn club, with a valuation of over $1 billion. The company has also acquired many other fantasy sports platforms like Halaplay, MyTeam11 and Fantain Sports.

The founders of Dream11 were able to identify a gap in the market and create a unique solution that resonated with Indian consumers. Their story serves as an inspiration for entrepreneurs and startups looking to build a successful business from scratch, especially in a highly regulated and complex industry.

ABOUT CRED

Cred is an Indian fintech company that operates through a subscription-based business model. The company offers a credit card bill payment platform for users, which helps them to manage and pay their credit card bills in a convenient and efficient manner. Cred generates revenue primarily through subscriptions and membership fees for its premium services. Users can choose to pay for a monthly or annual membership to access additional features and benefits such as credit score tracking, personalized financial advice, and exclusive deals and offers from partner merchants. Additionally, Cred also generates revenue through transaction fees charged to users for certain services, such as late fee waivers and balance transfer. The company also earns by collecting commission from the merchants for providing them with the customers.

FINTECH

Founder : Kunal Shah

Kunal Shah is an Indian entrepreneur and the founder of CRED, a credit card bill payment app that rewards users for paying their credit card bills on time. He is also the founder of Freecharge, one of India's first and largest mobile wallet and e-commerce platforms, which was later acquired by Snapdeal.

Kunal Shah started his career as a software engineer and later became an entrepreneur. He founded Freecharge in 2010, which grew to become one of India's largest mobile wallet and e-commerce platforms. In 2015, Freecharge was acquired by Snapdeal for an estimated $450 million.

After the successful exit from Freecharge, Kunal Shah decided to focus on the credit card industry and founded CRED in 2018. CRED's mission is to help people improve their credit scores and make it easier for them to access credit.

The app rewards users for paying their credit card bills on time, and also provides information and tools to help users manage their credit.

Kunal Shah faced several challenges in the early days of starting CRED. One of the major challenges was the lack of awareness and understanding about the importance of credit scores among Indian consumers. Additionally, building a reliable and efficient technology infrastructure to support the business was a significant challenge.

Despite these challenges, Kunal Shah persevered and focused on building a user-friendly platform that was easy for Indian consumers to use. He also invested in marketing and customer acquisition efforts to raise awareness about CRED among Indian consumers.

Through his hard work and determination, CRED has grown to become one of the leading credit card bill payment apps in India. The company has raised over $200 million in funding from investors such as Sequoia Capital, Ribbit Capital, and Tiger Global.

ABOUT UNACADEMY

Unacademy is an Indian online education platform that operates through a freemium and subscription-based business model. The company offers a wide range of educational content, including video lectures and practice tests, for students preparing for competitive exams such as the IAS and GATE. Unacademy generates revenue through multiple sources, primarily through subscriptions, live classes, personalized learning experiences and sponsored content. Users can access a certain amount of content for free but to access more advanced and specialized content, they need to pay for a monthly or annual subscription. The company aims to provide accessible and affordable education for students preparing for competitive exams, and its business model is based on offering a mix of free and paid content and services.

EDTECH

Founder : Gaurav Munjal, Roman Saini, and Hemesh Singh

Unacademy, an Indian online education technology company, was founded in 2010 by Gaurav Munjal, Roman Saini, and Hemesh Singh.

Gaurav Munjal, the CEO of Unacademy, is an engineering graduate from Delhi College of Engineering and has a background in technology. Before starting Unacademy, he had experience in the education industry and had worked as a teacher and tutor.

Roman Saini, the co-founder of Unacademy, is a medical doctor and an Indian Administrative Services (IAS) officer. He had experience in teaching and had taught students for Indian Civil Services Examination prior to starting Unacademy.

Hemesh Singh, the co-founder of Unacademy, is a graduate of Indian Institute of Technology (IIT) Delhi and has a background in technology. Prior to starting Unacademy.

The founders of Unacademy faced several challenges in the early days of starting the company. One of the main challenges was building a reliable and efficient technology platform to support the online courses and test preparation services. Additionally, they had to deal with the lack of awareness of online education in India. They also struggled to raise funding from investors as the online education market was relatively new at that time.

Despite these challenges, the founders of Unacademy persevered and focused on building a platform that was user-friendly, easy to navigate and provided a wide range of courses and test preparation services. They also invested in marketing and customer acquisition efforts to raise awareness about Unacademy among Indian students.

Through their hard work, determination, and a strong vision, Unacademy has grown to become one of the leading online education platforms in India. The company has raised over $200 million in funding from investors such as SoftBank, Facebook, and Sequoia Capital. Today, Unacademy has millions of registered users and is considered as one of the key players in the Indian online education market.

ABOUT DELHIVERY

Delhivery is an Indian logistics and supply chain management company that operates through a B2B business model. The company provides end-to-end logistics solutions for e-commerce companies and other businesses. Delhivery generates revenue through multiple sources, primarily through its delivery and logistics services. The company provides services such as warehousing, last-mile delivery, and cross-border transportation for its clients. Additionally, Delhivery also offers value-added services such as order fulfillment, inventory management, and reverse logistics. Delhivery has a large network of delivery partners and its own fleet of delivery vehicles, which help it to provide fast and reliable delivery services. The company's business model is based on providing efficient and cost-effective logistics solutions for e-commerce and other businesses, which help them to manage and streamline their supply chain operations.

LOGISTICS

Founder : Sahil Barua, Mohit Tandon, Bhavesh Manglani, Suraj Saharan, and Kapil Bharati

Delhivery, an Indian logistics and supply chain management company was founded in 2011 by Sahil Barua, Mohit Tandon, Bhavesh Manglani, Suraj Saharan, and Kapil Bharati.

Sahil Barua, the CEO of Delhivery, is a graduate of Indian Institute of Technology (IIT) Delhi and has a background in technology. Prior to starting Delhivery, he had experience in the logistics industry and had worked with companies such as FedEx. He saw an opportunity to create a logistics company that would make e-commerce delivery more efficient and reliable in India.

The founders of Delhivery faced several challenges in the early days of starting the company. They had to navigate the complexities of starting a logistics company in India, which had a reputation for being a difficult industry to operate in.

One of the main challenges was building a reliable and efficient supply chain to support the delivery of e-commerce orders. Additionally, they had to deal with the lack of technology infrastructure and low awareness of e-commerce in India. The founders also faced difficulties in raising funding from investors as the e-commerce market was relatively new at that time.

Despite these challenges, the founders of Delhivery persevered and focused on building a logistics network that was efficient, reliable and could handle the volume of e-commerce deliveries. They also invested in technology and automation to improve the efficiency of their operations. Through their hard work, determination and a strong vision, Delhivery has grown to become one of the leading logistics and supply chain management companies in India.

Today, the company serves more than 30,000 pin codes across India and has a network of over 3,000 cities and towns. It also has a fleet of more than 10,000 vehicles and over 30,000 employees.

ABOUT MEESHO

Meesho is an Indian e-commerce platform that operates through a social commerce business model. The company enables individuals, small businesses and entrepreneurs to start their own online stores and sell products through social media platforms such as WhatsApp, Facebook and Instagram. Meesho generates revenue through commissions on the sales made through its platform, from the resellers. Additionally, the company also earns revenue through advertising and sponsored content, where businesses can pay to promote their products on the platform. Meesho's business model is based on providing a simple and accessible way for individuals and small businesses to start their own online stores and sell products through social media. The platform also offers various tools and features to help resellers manage their stores, such as inventory management and order tracking, making it easy for anyone to start their own business.

ECOMMERCE

Founder : Vidit Aatrey and Sanjeev Barnwal

Meesho was founded in 2015 by IIT graduates Vidit Aatrey and Sanjeev Barnwal. They had the vision to empower millions of small businesses and entrepreneurs in India, by providing them with the tools and technology to sell their products online.

The company started with a small team and limited resources, but the founders were determined to make their vision a reality. They faced several challenges in the early days, such as lack of funding, competition from established e-commerce players, and the need to educate small businesses about the benefits of online selling.

Despite these challenges, the founders persevered and focused on building a user-friendly platform that was easy for small businesses to use. They also invested in marketing and customer acquisition efforts to raise awareness about Meesho among small businesses and entrepreneurs. The idea was to allows individuals to start their own businesses by reselling products on various social media platforms like WhatsApp, Facebook, and Instagram.

The company also introduced new features such as a mobile app and a supplier-to-consumer model, which helped to attract more resellers and customers to the platform. In addition to its success in India, Meesho has also begun to expand into other markets, such as Egypt and Indonesia. The company plans to use the funding it has raised to continue to expand its reach and improve its technology

Through their hard work and determination, Meesho has grown to become one of the leading social commerce platforms in India. The company has raised over $300 million in funding from investors such as Sequoia Capital, SAIF Partners, and Shunwei Capital. Today, Meesho has millions of registered users and more than 10 million small businesses and entrepreneurs using the platform.

The story of Meesho and its founders is a great example of how a small startup can overcome obstacles and achieve success through hard work, determination, and a strong vision. It serves as an inspiration for entrepreneurs and startups looking to build a successful business from scratch.

ABOUT AFFLE

Affle operates through a B2B business model and its business is to provide mobile advertising and analytics solutions to businesses. Affle generates revenue through multiple sources, primarily through its mobile advertising services. It uses its proprietary technology to provide targeted mobile advertising solutions to businesses. The company also provides analytics services such as audience profiling, campaign optimization and measurement. Additionally, Affle also provides mobile commerce solutions for businesses to create mobile-based shopping experiences for their customers. It's business model is based on providing mobile advertising and analytics solutions to businesses, which help them to reach and engage with their target audience more effectively and improve the ROI of their advertising campaigns.

ADTECH

Founder : Anuj Khanna Sohum

Affle is a mobile advertising and analytics company, founded in 2006 by Anuj Khanna Sohum. The company provides mobile advertising, data analytics, and consumer insights solutions to businesses and organizations.

Anuj Khanna Sohum, the founder and CEO of Affle, is a graduate of Indian Institute of Technology (IIT) Delhi and has a background in technology. Before starting Affle, he had experience in the mobile and internet industry and had worked with companies such as Microsoft and Samsung.

He saw an opportunity to create a mobile advertising and analytics company that would help businesses and organizations better understand and engage with mobile users.

The founder of Affle faced several challenges in the early days of starting the company. One of the main challenges was the lack of understanding and acceptance of mobile advertising and analytics among businesses and organizations. Additionally, the company had to deal with the lack of awareness and understanding of the importance of mobile advertising and analytics among consumers.

Despite these challenges, the founder of Affle persevered and focused on building a sustainable and profitable business model. He invested in research and development to improve the effectiveness and efficiency of the company's mobile advertising and analytics solutions. He also invested in marketing and customer acquisition efforts to raise awareness about Affle among businesses and organizations.

Through his hard work, determination, and a strong vision, Affle has grown to become one of the leading mobile advertising and analytics companies in Southeast Asia. The company has raised funding from investors such as Microsoft, Itochu and Qualcomm Ventures.

Today, Affle's solutions are used by businesses and organizations across Southeast Asia to better understand and engage with mobile users.

ABOUT ZIVAME

Zivame is an Indian online lingerie and innerwear store that operates through a e-commerce business model. The company sells a wide range of lingerie and innerwear products for women, including bras, panties, shapewear, and sleepwear. Zivame generates revenue through the sale of its products, which are purchased directly through its website. The company offers a wide variety of products from multiple brands, and also has its own private label. Zivame's business model is based on providing a convenient and discreet way for women to purchase lingerie and innerwear products online, with a focus on providing a wide range of sizes and styles to cater to different body types and preferences. They also offer free home delivery, free returns, and cash on delivery as the mode of payments.

E COMMERCE

Founder : Richa Kar

Richa Kar is an Indian entrepreneur and the founder of Zivame, an online lingerie and intimate wear retailer. She is a graduate of Indian Institute of Management (IIM) Bangalore, and has a background in business consulting before starting Zivame.

Richa Kar identified a gap in the Indian market for a dedicated online retailer for lingerie and intimate wear, as the category was largely ignored by traditional retailers, and buying these products in physical stores could be an uncomfortable and embarrassing experience for many women. She saw an opportunity to create a platform that would make it easier for Indian women to buy lingerie and intimate wear in a comfortable and discreet way.

In the early days of starting Zivame, Richa Kar faced several challenges. One of the major challenges was the lack of awareness and understanding about the benefits of online lingerie shopping among Indian consumers. Additionally, building a reliable and efficient technology infrastructure to support the business was a significant challenge.

Another major challenge was the lack of funding. Richa Kar had to bootstrap the company in the early days and struggled to raise funding from investors. She faced rejection after rejection, but she persisted and eventually was able to secure funding from some investors.

Through her hard work and determination, Zivame has grown to become one of the leading online lingerie and intimate wear retailers in India. The company has raised over $40 million in funding from investors such as IDG Ventures, Kalaari Capital, and Unilazer Ventures. Today, Zivame has millions of registered users and is considered as one of the key players in the Indian e-commerce market.

Richa Kar's story is a great example of how an entrepreneur can overcome many obstacles and achieve success through hard work, determination, and a strong vision. Her story serves as an inspiration for entrepreneurs and startups looking to build a successful business from scratch, particularly in a niche market. Richa Kar was able to identify a gap in the market and create a unique solution that resonated with Indian consumers.

ABOUT GROWW

Groww is an Indian investment platform that operates through a B2B and B2C business model. The company provides a platform for individuals to invest in mutual funds, stocks and other investment options in a seamless and easy way. Groww generates revenue through multiple sources, primarily through commissions on the investments made through its platform. Additionally, the company also earns revenue through other financial services such as stockbroking and wealth management. Groww's business model is based on providing a user-friendly and easy-to-use platform for individuals to invest in different financial products, and also educate them on various investment options. The platform also offers various tools and features to help users manage their investments, such as portfolio tracking and analytics, making it easy for anyone to start investing.

FINTECH

Founder : Lalit Keshre, Harsh Jain, Neeraj Singh, and Ishan Bansal

Groww was founded in 2017 by Lalit Keshre, Harsh Jain, Neeraj Singh, and Ishan Bansal.

All of them used to work at same company InMobi, Starting Groww was not easy, company faced lots of problem in starting days including Lack of awareness about online investing among Indian consumers, the main challenges was to educate and create awareness about the benefits of online investing among Indian consumers.

This was especially difficult as many people were still skeptical about the security and reliability of online investment platforms, Building a platform that could handle the large amount of data and transactions required for online investing was also a significant challenge for the founders. They had to ensure that the platform was secure and could handle a large number of users without any downtime.

Raising funds for a startup is also one of the biggest challenge, and the founders of Groww had to overcome this by pitching to various investors and venture capitalists. They had to convince them of the potential of their business and the market opportunity, Navigating the legal and regulatory complexities of operating in the financial services industry as financial services industry is heavily regulated, and the founders had to navigate the various legal and regulatory complexities of operating in this industry. This included obtaining the necessary licenses and approvals from regulatory bodies.

Despite these challenges, the founders of Groww persevered and focused on building a user-friendly platform that was easy for Indian consumers to use and understand. They also invested in marketing and customer acquisition efforts to raise awareness about Groww among Indian consumers.

Through their hard work, determination and a strong vision, Groww has grown to become one of the leading investment platforms in India.

ABOUT MAMAEARTH

Mamaearth is an Indian e-commerce company that specializes in selling natural and organic personal care and baby care products. Mamaearth operates through an e-commerce business model, generating revenue by selling its own brand of products on its website and other e-commerce platforms. Mamaearth's products are made from natural and organic ingredients, free from harmful chemicals and toxins, which are safe for babies and adults. The company's business model is based on providing a range of natural and organic personal care and baby care products that are free from harmful chemicals and toxins, and also making them accessible through e-commerce platforms. They also offer free home delivery, free returns, and cash on delivery as the mode of payments.

E COMMERCE

Founder : Varun and Ghazal Alagh

Mamaearth, an Indian baby and mother care brand, was founded in 2016 by husband-wife duo, Varun and Ghazal Alagh.

Varun Alagh, the CEO of Mamaearth, is a graduate of Indian Institute of Technology (IIT) Delhi and has a background in technology. Before starting Mamaearth, he had experience in the e-commerce industry and had worked with companies such as Justdial and Jabong. He saw an opportunity to create a brand that would provide safe and natural products for babies and mothers.

Ghazal Alagh, the COO of Mamaearth, is a graduate of Indian Institute of Technology (IIT) Delhi and has a background in marketing. Prior to starting Mamaearth, she had experience in the FMCG industry and had worked with companies such as P&G and Nestle. She brings a wealth of experience in marketing and product development to the company.

The founders of Mamaearth faced several challenges in the early days of starting the company, such as lack of awareness about the benefits of natural and toxin-free products among Indian consumers, difficulties in building a reliable and efficient supply chain to source natural ingredients, and struggle to raise funding from investors. Additionally, they had to navigate the complexities of operating in a highly competitive industry.

Despite these challenges, Varun and Ghazal Alagh persevered and focused on building a brand that was committed to providing safe and natural products for babies and mothers. They also invested in marketing and customer acquisition efforts to raise awareness about Mamaearth among Indian consumers.

Through their hard work, determination, and a strong vision, Mamaearth has grown to become one of the leading baby and mother care brands in India. The company has raised over $12 million in funding from investors such as Sequoia Capital, Fireside Ventures and Saama Capital. Today, Mamaearth is considered as one of the key players in the Indian baby and mother care market.

ABOUT RAPIDO

Rapido is an Indian bike-taxi service provider. It operates through a transportation network company business model. Rapido connects customers with nearby bike-taxi drivers through its mobile application. The company generates revenue by taking a commission from the fare paid by customers for each ride. Rapido's business model is based on providing a convenient, affordable, and quick transportation service to customers using bike-taxis. The company uses a GPS-enabled mobile application to connect customers with nearby bike-taxi drivers, making it easy for customers to book a ride in real-time. Rapido also provides driver partners with a mobile app to manage their business and track their earnings. The company also offers safety features such as real-time tracking, in-app customer support, and driver ratings to ensure the safety of its riders.

BIKE TAXI

Founder : Aravind Sanka, Pavan Guntupalli and Rishikesh SR

Rapido is an Indian on-demand bike taxi platform. The company was founded in 2015 by Aravind Sanka, Pavan Guntupalli and Rishikesh SR.

Aravind Sanka, the Co-Founder and CEO of Rapido, is a graduate of Indian Institute of Technology (IIT) Madras and has a background in technology. Before starting Rapido, he had experience in the software industry and had worked with companies such as Microsoft, Cisco and Verifone.

Founders saw an opportunity to create an on-demand bike taxi platform that would make transportation more accessible and affordable for Indian consumers, but their journey was full of hurdles.

The founders of Rapido faced several challenges in the early days of starting the company. One of the main challenges was building a reliable and efficient platform for bike taxi service and attracting customers in a market that was dominated by traditional taxi services.

Additionally, the bike taxi industry was still at a nascent stage and the lack of awareness and understanding about the concept among the general public and investors was a major hurdle. They also struggled to raise funding from investors as the bike taxi market was relatively new and not well-established in India at that time.

Despite these challenges and tough competiton from Ola and Uber, the founders of Rapido persevered and focused on building a platform that would provide a more efficient and effective way for people to commute in cities. They invested in research and development, and in building a strong team of experts in the field.

Through their hard work, determination, and a strong vision, Rapido has grown to become one of the leading bike taxi platforms in India. The company has millions of registered users and is considered as one of the key players in the Indian bike taxi market.

ABOUT DELTA CORP

Delta Corp Limited is an Indian gaming and hospitality company. The company operates through a B2C business model, generating revenue through its casino and gaming operations, as well as its hospitality business. The company owns and operates several casinos and gaming properties in India, as well as hotels, resorts and other hospitality properties. Delta Corp's business model is based on providing gaming and hospitality services to customers. The company's casinos and gaming properties offer a wide range of games and activities, including slot machines, table games, and live entertainment. Additionally, the company's hospitality properties provide customers with accommodation and other amenities, such as restaurants and spas. They also have online gaming and poker business through their subsidiary Gaussian Networks Private Limited.

CASINO

Founder : Jaydev Mody

Delta Corp is an Indian gaming and hospitality company that was founded in 2007 by Jaydev Mody.

Jaydev Mody, the founder of Delta Corp, is a businessman and entrepreneur. He holds a degree in Commerce from the University of Mumbai. Before starting Delta Corp, he had experience in the real estate and construction industry and had worked with companies such as the K Raheja Group and the Hiranandani Group. He saw an opportunity to create a company that would focus on the gaming and hospitality industry in India, which was still at a nascent stage.

The founder of Delta Corp faced several challenges in the early days of starting the company. One of the main challenges was to establish the company's credibility and attract customers in a market that was dominated by established players.

Additionally, the gaming and hospitality sector was still not well-established in India, and there was a lack of awareness and understanding about the industry among the general public and investors. He also struggled to raise funding from investors as the gaming and hospitality market was relatively new and not well-established in India at that time.

Despite these challenges, the founder of Delta Corp persevered and focused on building a company that would provide innovative solutions in the gaming and hospitality industry. He invested in research and development and in building a strong team of experts in the field.

Through his hard work, determination, and a strong vision, Delta Corp has grown to become one of the leading gaming and hospitality companies in India.

The company owns and operates several casinos, hotels, and resorts across the country. Delta Corp has also been recognized for its contributions to the gaming and hospitality industry and has received several awards and accolades.

ABOUT MOBIKWIK

MobiKwik is an Indian digital wallet and financial services provider. The company operates through a B2C business model, generating revenue by offering a range of financial services to customers through its mobile application. The services offered by MobiKwik include utility bill payments, and online shopping. The company's business model is based on providing customers with a simple and convenient way to access various financial services through their mobile phone. MobiKwik's mobile application allows customers to pay bills, recharge their mobile phones, and make other transactions, all from the convenience of their mobile device. The company also earns revenue through commissions and fees on transactions made through its platform, as well as through interest on the money held in customer's digital wallets. Additionally, the company also provides its services to merchants, enabling them to accept payments, disburse payments and also to provide loyalty schemes to their customers

FINTECH

Founder : Bipin Preet Singh and Upasana Taku

MobiKwik, an Indian mobile wallet and e-commerce platform, was founded in 2009 by Bipin Preet Singh and Upasana Taku.

Bipin Preet Singh, a serial entrepreneur and technologist, has a degree in Computer Science and has worked with companies such as Oracle and Yahoo before starting MobiKwik. He has over a decade of experience in the technology industry and has always been passionate about building innovative technology solutions for Indian consumers.

Upasana Taku, an engineer and an MBA from IIM Ahmedabad, has over a decade of experience in the financial services industry, having worked with companies such as American Express, Standard Chartered and GE Money. She has a deep understanding of the Indian financial system and the challenges that consumers face in accessing financial services.

The founders of MobiKwik brought together their complementary skills and experiences to create a unique and innovative solution to help Indian consumers access online payments and e-commerce in a simple and convenient way.

In the early days, Bipin Preet Singh and Upasana Taku faced several challenges such as lack of awareness about mobile wallets among Indian consumers, difficulty in building a reliable and efficient technology infrastructure, and struggle to raise funding from investors. They had to bootstrap the company in the early days and struggled to raise funding from investors. But despite these obstacles, they persevered and focused on building a user-friendly platform that was easy for Indian consumers to use. They also invested in marketing and customer acquisition efforts to raise awareness about MobiKwik among Indian consumers.

Through their hard work, determination and vision, MobiKwik has grown to become one of the leading mobile wallet and e-commerce platforms in India. The company has raised over $150 million in funding from big fishes.

ABOUT MPL

MPL (Mobile Premier League) is an Indian mobile gaming platform. It operates through a freemium business model, providing users with free-to-play mobile games and generating revenue through in-app purchases, paid subscriptions, and advertising. MPL's business model is based on providing a wide range of mobile games to users, spanning various genres such as sports, puzzle, action, and more. Users can play these games for free, but MPL generates revenue by offering in-app purchases and paid subscriptions that enhance the gaming experience. Users can also participate in tournaments and win cash prizes, and MPL takes a commission on these transactions. They also generate revenue by displaying ads in-game and through brand partnerships. Additionally, the company also provides its services to game developers, enabling them to monetize their games and make them available to a large user base.

GAMING

Founder : Sai Srinivas Kiran G and Shubham Malhotra

Mobile Premier League (MPL) was founded in 2018 by Sai Srinivas Kiran G and Shubham Malhotra.

Sai Srinivas Kiran G, the CEO of MPL, is a graduate of Indian Institute of Technology (IIT) Delhi and has a background in technology. Before starting MPL, he had experience in the mobile gaming industry and had worked with companies such as Play Games24x7 and Nazara Technologies. He saw an opportunity to create a platform that would bring the excitement of esports and online gaming to a larger audience in India.

Shubham Malhotra, the COO of MPL, is a graduate of Indian Institute of Management (IIM) Calcutta, and has a background in finance. Prior to starting MPL, he had experience in the mobile gaming industry and had worked with companies such as Hike and InMobi. He brings a wealth of experience in business development and operations to the company.

The founders of MPL faced several challenges in the early days of starting the company, such as lack of awareness about the concept of mobile gaming and esports in India, difficulties in building a reliable and efficient technology infrastructure to support the business, and struggle to raise funding from investors. Additionally, they had to navigate the legal complexities of operating in a highly regulated industry.

Despite these challenges, Sai Srinivas Kiran G and Shubham Malhotra persevered and focused on building a user-friendly platform that was easy for Indian users to use. They also invested in marketing and customer acquisition efforts to raise awareness about MPL among Indian consumers.

Through their hard work, determination, and a strong vision, MPL has grown to become one of the leading mobile gaming platforms in India. The company has raised over $95 million in funding from investors such as Sequoia Capital, Times Internet, and RTP Global. Today, MPL has millions of registered users and is considered as one of the key players in the Indian gaming market.

ABOUT PHARMEASY

Pharmeasy is an Indian online pharmacy platform. It operates through a B2C business model, providing customers with a convenient way to purchase medicines and health products online, and generating revenue through the sale of these products. Pharmeasy's business model is based on providing customers with a wide range of medicines and health products, including prescription drugs and over-the-counter medicines, as well as health supplements and personal care products. Customers can order these products through the Pharmeasy mobile app or website, and the company delivers the products directly to the customer's doorstep. Pharmeasy also provides a subscription-based service for repeat medicines, where customers can opt for regular delivery of their prescribed medicines. The company also generates revenue by providing a platform for other healthcare services like online consultation, home diagnostic test and booking of doctor appointment.

E COMMERCE

Founder : Dharmil Sheth and Dhaval Shah

PharmEasy, an Indian online pharmacy and healthcare platform company, was founded in 2015 by Dharmil Sheth and Dhaval Shah.

Dharmil Sheth, the CEO of PharmEasy, is a graduate of Indian Institute of Technology (IIT) Bombay and has a background in technology. Before starting PharmEasy, he had experience in the healthcare industry and had worked with companies such as Practo and Cipla. He saw an opportunity to create an platform that would make healthcare more accessible and convenient for Indian consumers.

Dhaval Shah, the COO of PharmEasy, is a graduate of Indian Institute of Technology (IIT) Bombay and has a background in technology. Prior to starting PharmEasy, he had experience in the healthcare industry and had worked with companies such as Practo and Cipla. He brings expertise in operations and supply chain management to the company.

The founders of PharmEasy faced several challenges in the early days of starting the company, such as lack of awareness about the benefits of online ordering of medicines among Indian consumers, difficulties in building a reliable and efficient supply chain to source medicines, and struggle to raise funding from investors. Additionally, they had to navigate the complexities of operating in a highly regulated industry.

Despite these challenges, Dharmil Sheth and Dhaval Shah persevered and focused on building a platform that was committed to providing safe, accessible and affordable healthcare for Indian consumers. They also invested in marketing and customer acquisition efforts to raise awareness about PharmEasy among Indian consumers.

Through their hard work, determination, and a strong vision, PharmEasy has grown to become one of the leading online pharmacy and healthcare platforms in India. The company has raised over $120 million in funding from investors such as Sequoia Capital, Nexus Venture Partners, and Temasek. Today, PharmEasy has millions of registered users and is considered as one of the key players in the Indian healthcare market.

ABOUT LENSKART

Lenskart is an Indian e-commerce company that specializes in eyewear and eye-care products. It operates through a B2C business model, providing customers with a wide range of eyewear products, including eyeglasses, sunglasses, contact lenses, and eye-care solutions. Lenskart generates revenue by selling these products to customers through its online platform, as well as through physical stores. The company's business model is based on providing customers with a convenient and hassle-free way to shop for eyewear products, with features like home trial, virtual try-on, and easy return policy. Lenskart also offers eye-care services such as eye check-up and eye consultation through its network of partner optometrists, and generates revenue from these services as well. Additionally, the company also generates revenue through partnerships with other companies and brands, and through advertising and sponsored content.

E COMMERCE

Founder : Peyush Bansal

Lenskart, an Indian online eyewear retailer, was founded in 2010 by Peyush Bansal.

Peyush Bansal, the founder of Lenskart, is a graduate of Indian Institute of Technology (IIT) Delhi and has a background in technology. Before starting Lenskart, he had experience in the e-commerce industry and had worked with companies such as Indiamart and Indiatimes. He saw an opportunity to create an online platform that would make eyewear more accessible and affordable for Indian consumers.

The founder of Lenskart, Peyush Bansal, faced several challenges in the early days of starting the company. One of the main challenges was building a reliable and efficient supply chain to source eyewear products. Additionally, he had to deal with the lack of awareness of e-commerce and online shopping in India. He also struggled to raise funding from investors as the e-commerce market was relatively new at that time.

Despite these challenges, Peyush Bansal persevered and focused on building a platform that was user-friendly, easy to navigate and provided a wide range of eyewear products. He also invested in marketing and customer acquisition efforts to raise awareness about Lenskart among Indian consumers.

Through his hard work, determination, and a strong vision, Lenskart has grown to become one of the leading online eyewear retailers in India. The company has raised over $160 million in funding from investors such as TPG Growth, IDG Ventures, and IFC. Today, Lenskart has millions of registered users and is considered as one of the key players in the Indian eyewear market.

The company has also expanded to offline retail by opening over 500 stores across India. Peyush Bansal's entrepreneurial journey was not a smooth one, he faced several challenges and obstacles but his determination and a strong vision to make eyewear more accessible and affordable for Indian consumers helped him to overcome all the difficulties and build a successful company.

ABOUT RIVIGO

Rivigo is an Indian logistics and supply chain management company. It operates through a B2B and B2C business model, providing customers with a wide range of logistics and supply chain management services, including transportation, warehousing, and distribution services. Rivigo generates revenue by providing these services to businesses, such as manufacturers and retailers, as well as to individual customers. The company's business model is based on providing customers with a reliable, efficient, and cost-effective way to manage their logistics and supply chain needs. Rivigo utilizes technology to improve operational efficiency and reduce transit times, and also provides real-time tracking and visibility of consignments. Additionally, the company also generates revenue through partnerships with other companies and through its logistics infrastructure.

LOGISTICS

Founder : Deepak Garg and Gazal Kalra

Rivigo, an Indian logistics and transportation company, was founded in 2014 by Deepak Garg and Gazal Kalra.

Deepak Garg, the CEO of Rivigo, is a graduate of Indian Institute of Technology (IIT) Kanpur and has a background in technology. Before starting Rivigo, he worked in the logistics industry and had experience in companies such as McKinsey & Company and Excel Crop Care. He saw an opportunity to create a transportation company that would make long-haul trucking more efficient and reliable in India.

Gazal Kalra, the co-founder of Rivigo, is a graduate of Indian Institute of Technology (IIT) Delhi and has a background in technology. Prior to starting Rivigo, she worked in the logistics industry and had experience in companies such as McKinsey & Company and Excel Crop Care.

The founders of Rivigo faced several challenges in the early days of starting the company. They had to navigate the complexities of starting a logistics company in India, which had a reputation for being a difficult industry to operate in. One of the main challenges was building a reliable and efficient transportation network to support the delivery of goods. Additionally, they had to deal with the lack of technology infrastructure and low awareness of e-commerce in India. The founders also faced difficulties in raising funding from investors as the logistics market was relatively new at that time.

Despite these challenges, the founders of Rivigo persevered and focused on building a transportation network that was efficient, reliable, and could handle the volume of goods delivery. They also invested in technology and automation to improve the efficiency of their operations. Through their hard work, determination, and a strong vision, Rivigo has grown to become one of the leading logistics and transportation companies in India. Today, the company serves more than 10,000 pin codes across India and has a fleet of more than 6,000 vehicles and over 10,000 employees and now being sold to Mahindra Logistics.

ABOUT UPSTOX

Upstox is an Indian online brokerage firm that provides trading and investment services. It operates through a B2C business model, providing customers with a platform to trade in different financial instruments such as equities, derivatives, currencies and commodities. Upstox generates revenue through brokerage charges and other transactional charges for trades executed on its platform. The company's business model is based on providing low-cost, easy-to-use, and accessible trading and investment services to retail investors. Upstox uses technology to automate and simplify the trading process, and also provides research and education resources to help customers make informed investment decisions. Additionally, the company also generates revenue through partnerships with other financial service providers and by providing access to other financial products such as mutual funds.

FINTECH

Founder : Ravi Kumar, Kunal Varma and Ritesh Cashew

Upstox was founded in 2011 by Ravi Kumar, Kunal Varma and Ritesh Cashew.

Ravi Kumar, the CEO of Upstox, is a graduate of Indian Institute of Technology (IIT) Delhi and has a background in technology. Before starting Upstox, he had experience in the financial services industry and had worked with companies such as Oracle Financial Services and ICICI Direct. He saw an opportunity to create an online stockbroker that would make investing and trading more accessible and affordable for Indian consumers.

Kunal Varma, Co-Founder, CTO, and COO of Upstox, is a graduate of Indian Institute of Technology (IIT) Delhi and has a background in technology. Prior to starting Upstox, he had experience in the financial services industry and had worked with companies such as Oracle Financial Services and ICICI Direct.

The founders of Upstox faced several challenges in the early days of starting the company. One of the main challenges was building a reliable and efficient technology platform to support the trading and investment services. Additionally, they had to deal with the lack of awareness of online investing and trading in India. They also struggled to raise funding from investors as the online trading market was relatively new at that time.

Despite these challenges, the founders of Upstox persevered and focused on building a platform that was user-friendly, easy to navigate and provided a wide range of investment and trading services. They also invested in marketing and customer acquisition efforts to raise awareness about Upstox among Indian consumers.

Through their hard work, determination, and a strong vision, Upstox has grown to become one of the leading online stockbrokers in India. The company has raised over $120 million in funding from investors such as Tiger Global, Kalaari Capital, and GVK Davix. Today, Upstox has millions of registered users and is considered as one of the key players in the Indian online trading market.

ABOUT CURE FIT

Curefit is an Indian health and wellness company that provides a range of products and services to help customers improve their physical and mental well-being. It operates through a B2C business model, providing customers with a platform that offers a combination of fitness, food, and mental well-being services. Curefit generates revenue by selling its products and services, such as fitness classes, healthy food, and mental wellness programs. The company's business model is based on providing an integrated and personalized approach to health and wellness, by providing customers with access to a wide range of services through a single platform. Curefit uses technology to personalize the customer experience and provide customized recommendations, and also provides a community-based approach to wellness that encourages social interaction and support. Additionally, the company also generates revenue through partnerships with other health and wellness providers and by providing access to health insurance and services.

FITNESS

Founder : Mukesh Bansal and Ankit Nagori

CureFit, an Indian healthcare and wellness company, was founded in 2016 by Mukesh Bansal and Ankit Nagori.

Mukesh Bansal, the Co-founder and CEO of CureFit, is an engineering graduate from Indian Institute of Technology (IIT) Delhi and has a background in technology. Before starting CureFit, he had experience in the e-commerce industry and had worked with companies such as Flipkart and Myntra. He saw an opportunity to create a healthcare and wellness company that would make fitness and nutrition more accessible and affordable for Indian consumers.

Ankit Nagori, the Co-Founder of Curefit, is a Commerce graduate from St. Xavier's College, Kolkata and has a background in finance. Prior to starting Curefit, he had experience in the e-commerce industry and had worked with companies such as Flipkart and Myntra.

The founders of CureFit faced several challenges in the early days of starting the company. One of the main challenges was building a reliable and efficient supply chain to source and deliver the fitness and wellness products. Additionally, they had to deal with the lack of awareness of e-commerce and online shopping in India. They also struggled to raise funding from investors as the health and wellness market was relatively new at that time.

Despite these challenges, the founders of CureFit persevered and focused on building a platform that was user-friendly, easy to navigate and provided a wide range of fitness and wellness products and services. They also invested in marketing and customer acquisition efforts to raise awareness about CureFit among Indian consumers.

Through their hard work, determination, and a strong vision, CureFit has grown to become one of the leading healthcare and wellness companies in India. The company has raised over $200 million in funding from investors such as Accel Partners, IDG Ventures, and Kalaari Capital. Today, CureFit has millions of registered users and is considered as one of the key players in the Indian healthcare and wellness market. The company has also expanded to other countries such as Singapore, and Indonesia.

ABOUT RENEW POWER

ReNew Power is an Indian renewable energy company that focuses on developing, building, and operating clean energy projects. It operates through a B2B business model, providing customers with a range of clean energy solutions such as solar and wind power. ReNew Power generates revenue by selling the electricity generated by its clean energy projects to customers such as utilities, commercial and industrial customers and government agencies. The company's business model is based on providing sustainable, reliable and cost-effective renewable energy solutions to its customers. ReNew Power uses technology to optimize the performance of its clean energy projects, and also provides project development, engineering, procurement and construction services to its customers. Additionally, the company also generates revenue through partnerships with other renewable energy companies and by providing access to other clean energy products such as electric vehicles charging stations.

RENEWABLE ENERGY

Founder : Sumant Sinha

Renew Power, an Indian renewable energy company, was founded in 2011 by Sumant Sinha.

Sumant Sinha, the founder and Chairman of Renew Power, is a graduate of Indian Institute of Technology (IIT) Delhi and Indian Institute of Management (IIM) Ahmedabad. He has a background in finance and has worked with companies such as American Express and the National Thermal Power Corporation (NTPC) before starting Renew Power. He saw an opportunity to create a renewable energy company that would help reduce the dependence on fossil fuels in India.

The founder of Renew Power faced several challenges in the early days of starting the company. One of the main challenges was raising funding from investors as the renewable energy market was relatively new in India.

Additionally, the company had to deal with the lack of awareness and understanding of renewable energy among Indian consumers and the government. The company also faced challenges in terms of acquiring land and obtaining necessary permits for building power plants.

Despite these challenges, the founder of Renew Power persevered and focused on building a sustainable and profitable business model. He also invested in research and development to keep the company at the forefront of renewable energy technology. He also invested in marketing and customer acquisition efforts to raise awareness about Renew Power among Indian consumers.

Through his hard work, determination, and a strong vision, Renew Power has grown to become one of the leading renewable energy companies in India. The company has raised over $1 billion in funding from investors such as Goldman Sachs, Abu Dhabi Investment Authority, and Global Environment Fund. Today, Renew Power has over 10 GW of renewable energy assets under management and is considered as one of the key players in the Indian renewable energy market.

ABOUT MAP MY INDIA

MapmyIndia is an Indian company that provides mapping, navigation and location-based services. It operates through a B2B and B2C business model, providing customers with a range of mapping, navigation and location-based services, such as digital maps, GPS navigation, location-based analytics, and location-based advertising. MapmyIndia generates revenue by selling its products and services to customers such as businesses, governments, and individual consumers. The company's business model is based on providing accurate, up-to-date, and detailed mapping and location-based services to its customers. MapmyIndia uses technology to create and maintain digital maps and provide location-based services, and also provides a range of location-based analytics and advertising solutions to its customers. Additionally, the company also generates revenue through partnerships with other companies in the mapping and location-based services industry, and by providing access to GIS and geospatial data.

MAP AS A SERVICE

Founder : Rakesh Verma

MapmyIndia is an Indian mapping and location-based services company, founded in 1992 by Rakesh Verma.

Rakesh Verma, the founder and CEO of MapmyIndia, is a graduate of Delhi College of Engineering. He has a background in engineering and has worked with companies such as Indian Space Research Organisation (ISRO) and Bharat Electronics Limited (BEL) before starting MapmyIndia. He saw an opportunity to create a mapping and location-based services company that would help improve the accuracy and availability of digital maps in India.

The founder of MapmyIndia faced several challenges in the early days of starting the company. One of the main challenges was the lack of accurate and comprehensive digital maps of India.

Additionally, the company had to deal with the lack of awareness and understanding of the importance of digital maps and location-based services among Indian businesses and government agencies. The company also faced challenges in terms of acquiring data and obtaining necessary permits for mapping and surveying.

Despite these challenges, the founder of MapmyIndia persevered and focused on building a sustainable and profitable business model. He invested in research and development to improve the accuracy and coverage of the company's digital maps. He also invested in marketing and customer acquisition efforts to raise awareness about MapmyIndia among Indian businesses and government agencies.

Through his hard work, determination, and a strong vision, MapmyIndia has grown to become one of the leading mapping and location-based services companies in India. The company has raised funding from investors such as Qualcomm Ventures and Indian Angel Network. Today, MapmyIndia has a wide range of products and services, including digital maps, GPS navigation, and location-based services, that are used by businesses, government agencies, and individuals across India.

ABOUT RATE GAIN

RateGain is a software company that provides revenue management and pricing solutions for the travel and hospitality industry. It operates through a SaaS business model, providing customers with a range of software solutions for revenue management, pricing optimization, and distribution. RateGain generates revenue by selling its software solutions to customers such as hotels, airlines, online travel agencies, and vacation rental companies. The company's business model is based on providing advanced software solutions to improve revenue management and pricing strategies for its customers. RateGain uses technology such as artificial intelligence and machine learning to optimize pricing and revenue management for its customers, and also provides services such as data analytics, business intelligence and strategic consulting.

TOURISM

Founder : Bhanu Chopra

RateGain was founded in 2005 by Bhanu Chopra.

Bhanu Chopra, the founder and CEO of RateGain, is a graduate of Indian Institute of Technology (IIT) Delhi and has a background in technology. Before starting RateGain, he had experience in the travel and hospitality industry and had worked with companies such as American Airlines and Sabre. He saw an opportunity to create a revenue management and e-distribution solutions for the hospitality and travel industry that would help hotels, airlines, and online travel agencies better understand and manage their pricing and inventory.

The founder of RateGain faced several challenges in the early days of starting the company. One of the main challenges was the lack of understanding and acceptance of revenue management and e-distribution solutions among hotels, airlines, and online travel agencies. Additionally, the company had to deal with the lack of awareness and understanding of the importance of these solutions among customers.

Despite these challenges, the founder of RateGain persevered and focused on building a sustainable and profitable business model. He invested in research and development to improve the effectiveness and efficiency of the company's revenue management and e-distribution solutions. He also invested in marketing and customer acquisition efforts to raise awareness about RateGain among hotels, airlines, and online travel agencies.

Through his hard work, determination, and a strong vision, RateGain has grown to become one of the leading companies in the hospitality and travel industry providing revenue management, e-distribution, and channel management solutions. The company has raised funding from investors such as Norwest Venture Partners, Nexus Venture Partners, and Goldman Sachs. Today, RateGain's solutions are used by thousands of hotels, airlines and online travel agencies worldwide to better understand and manage their pricing and inventory.

ABOUT UPGRAD

UpGrad is an Indian edtech company that provides online education and professional development courses. It operates through a subscription-based business model, providing customers with access to a range of online courses and programs in areas such as technology, management, and data science. UpGrad generates revenue by selling subscriptions to its courses and programs to customers such as individual learners and corporations. The company's business model is based on providing accessible, high-quality, and industry-relevant education to its customers. UpGrad uses technology such as video lectures, interactive quizzes, and online discussion forums to deliver its courses and programs, and also provides support services such as mentorship, career guidance and networking opportunities. Additionally, the company also generates revenue through partnerships with universities, employers and industry experts to provide certifications and placements for its students.

ED TECH

Founder : Ronnie Screwvala, Mayank Kumar and Phalgun Kompalli

UpGrad was founded in 2015 by Ronnie Screwvala, Mayank Kumar and Phalgun Kompalli.

Ronnie Screwvala, the Co-Founder and Chairman of UpGrad, is a well-known entrepreneur and philanthropist in India. He is the founder of UTV Group, a media and entertainment company and also served as its CEO. He has a background in media and entertainment and has worked with companies such as Walt Disney and STAR India before starting UpGrad. He saw an opportunity to create an education technology company that would make higher education more accessible and affordable for Indian students.

Mayank Kumar, the Co-Founder and CEO of UpGrad, is a graduate of Indian Institute of Technology (IIT) Delhi and has a background in technology.

Phalgun Kompalli, the Co-Founder of UpGrad, is a graduate of Indian Institute of Technology (IIT) Delhi and has a background in technology.

The founders of UpGrad faced several challenges in the early days of starting the company. One of the main challenges was building a reliable and efficient technology platform for online and blended learning. Additionally, they had to deal with the lack of awareness and understanding of online and blended learning among Indian students and employers. They also struggled to raise funding from investors as the education technology market was relatively new in India.

Despite these challenges, the founders of UpGrad persevered and focused on building a platform that was user-friendly, easy to navigate and provided a wide range of online and blended learning programs. They also invested in marketing and customer acquisition efforts to raise awareness about UpGrad among Indian students and employers.

Through their hard work, determination, and a strong vision, UpGrad has grown to become one of the leading education technology companies in India. The company has raised over $120 million in funding from investors such as Sequoia Capital, SAIF Partners, and Kaizen Private Equity.

ABOUT FIRST CRY

FirstCry is an Indian e-commerce platform for baby products and children's clothing. It operates through an online marketplace business model, providing customers with a wide range of products from various brands. FirstCry generates revenue by taking a commission on the sale of products listed on its website. The company's business model is based on providing a one-stop-shop for parents to purchase all their baby and children's needs. FirstCry uses technology such as personalized product recommendations and targeted marketing to attract customers and increase sales. Additionally, the company also generates revenue through partnerships with brands, offering them a platform to reach a wider customer base and sell their products. FirstCry also offers multiple payment options and delivery services to the customer which makes it more convenient for them to shop.

E COMMERCE

Founder : Supam Maheshwari and Amitava Saha

FirstCry was established in 2010 by Supam Maheshwari and Amitava Saha. Both Co-Founders have an educational background from Indian Institute of Technology (IIT) Kanpur and have experience in the e-commerce and internet industry, having previously worked for companies such as McKinsey and Naukri.com.

The idea behind the creation of the platform was to make baby and children's products more accessible and affordable for Indian consumers.

In the early days of the company, the founders faced several challenges, including building a reliable supply chain, lack of awareness and understanding of e-commerce and online shopping in India, and difficulty in obtaining funding from investors due to the relatively new market. Despite these obstacles, the founders persevered by creating a user-friendly platform with a wide range of baby and children's products, and investing in marketing and customer acquisition efforts.

As the company grew, it expanded its product offerings to include a wider range of baby and children's products, including clothing, footwear, toys, and even maternity products. It also started to offer services such as online doctor consultations and vaccination booking.

In the following years, FirstCry continued to attract investment from prominent venture capital firms such as SoftBank, IDG Ventures, and Vertex Ventures. This helped the company to expand its reach and increase its customer base.

Today, FirstCry has millions of registered users and is considered one of the key players in the Indian baby and children's products market. It continues to innovate and expand its offerings to meet the changing needs of its customers.

Source Internet

www.ingramcontent.com/pod-product-compliance
Lightning Source LLC
Chambersburg PA
CBHW050257220526
45465CB00002B/715